FORMULA ONE 2018

Written by Graham Muncie

Designed by Duncan Cook Drummond

A Pillar Box Red Publication

© 2017. Published by Pillar Box Red Publishing Limited, in association with The Daily Mirror. Printed in the EU.

This is an independent publication. It has no connection with the organisation(s), personality, or personalities associated to the sport featured, or with any organisation or individual connected in any way whatsoever with the organisation(s) or personality or personalities featured.

Any quotes within this publication which are attributed to a personality, or personalities associated with the sport featured have been sourced from other publications, or from the internet, and, as such, are a matter of public record. They have not been given directly to the author.

Whilst every effort has been made to ensure the accuracy of information within this publication, the publisher shall have no liability to any person or entity with respect to any inaccuracy, misleading information, loss or damage caused directly or indirectly by the information contained within this book.

The views expressed are solely those of the author and do not reflect the opinions of Pillar Box Red Publishing Limited or the Daily Mirror. All rights reserved.

ISBN 978-1-907823-89-3

Images © PA Images.

D1346484

CONTENTS

Ruling the Roost
Meet the Current Champion

NICO
ROSBERG

Factfile

Date of Birth: 27th June 1985

Born: Wiesbaden, Germany

Best-Ever Championship Finish: World Champion 2016

Current Team: Retired

GERMAN-BORN STAR NICO ROSBERG achieved a lifetime ambition when he was crowned Formula 1 World Champion in 2016. An exciting finale to the season saw Rosberg clinch the title by the slimmest margin of five points. There was no shortage of controversy in this last race as Rosberg's team partner, Lewis Hamilton, attempted to slow the race down to allow the opposition to catch them. However, Rosberg was not to be put off by this and he recorded the second place required to claim his first ever World Championship.

The Formula 1 world was then shocked when, having completed what he felt was his destiny, Rosberg announced he was to retire from racing.

Personal Life

It could be said that Rosberg was destined to be a Formula 1 racer from the day he was born, as he is the son of a former World Champion, Keke Rosberg. In fact, Nico was born just four days after his dad raced to victory in the 1985 United States Grand Prix. Raised in Monaco and still residing there to this day, Rosberg is fluent in five languages and is married to his childhood friend Vivian Sibold, with whom he has one child.

Racing Career

Rosberg started his racing career at the age of six when he took up go-karting, before moving to the German Formula BMW series as a 17 year old. A quick progression to Formula 2 was to follow and Rosberg was the first ever champion at that level in 2005. This propelled the German into the minds of Formula 1 teams and he was quickly snapped up by the Williams team for the 2006 season.

Rosberg made an immediate impact as he finished in the points and recorded the fastest lap of the race in his debut Grand Prix in Bahrain. This was to be as good as things got in that first season though, as he finished with four points for his efforts in what was not an overly-competitive Williams car.

The next couple of years were to be noted as solid improvement for Rosberg as he made a name for himself as a consistent point scorer, although that elusive first race win was yet to come.

In 2010 Rosberg was to move to Mercedes and this is where his career would take off; 15 point finishes in his first season was good enough for a Seventh Place finish in the Championship and Rosberg was starting to make people take note. 2011 was another consistent season and seventh place in the Championship was his once again.

2012 was the year that Rosberg was to take the chequered flag for the first time as he converted his pole position into first place in the Chinese Grand Prix.

2013 saw Lewis Hamilton join Mercedes as Rosberg's teammate and 4 years of intense rivalry was to follow. After a year of improvement for both in 2013, the battle was on-going into 2014.

Rosberg was to have his best-ever season to date that year finishing with five race wins; 15 podium finishes; 11 pole positions, as well as recording the fastest lap of a race five times. However, this was not enough to clinch the Championship, as Hamilton took the crown by a convincing 67 points.

2015 was to be a carbon copy of this as Rosberg again performed well but was to be bested by his Mercedes teammate. Rosberg did close the gap though, and the battle was set for the 2016 season.

Rosberg started in fantastic form, racing to victory in each of the first 4 races. He was to add five more race wins over the course of the season as he took his one and only World Championship before deciding to call time on his illustrious career.

Rosberg finished his career with a total of 23 race wins in Formula 1 which ranks him as the 12th All-Time Champion in the history of the sport.

If Anyone Can, Hamilton Can

LEWIS HAMILTON

Factfile

Date of Birth: 7th January 1985

Born: Stevenage, England

Best-Ever Championship Finish: World Champion 2008, 2014, 2015

Current Team: Mercedes

BRITISH SUPERSTAR LEWIS HAMILTON is one of the top men in the sport having been crowned World Champion on no less than three occasions. Hamilton is one of the greatest drivers of all time as he currently has the second most race wins in the history of Formula 1 and, at only 32 years old, the Stevenage-born racer is showing no signs of slowing down as he hunts down further world championships to cement his place in the history of the sport.

Racing Career

Like many, Hamilton started his racing career in the go-karting circuits at the tender age of eight years old. Hamilton's talent was there for all to see as he was British Champion by the age of ten. At 13 years old, then-McLaren team boss Ron Dennis spotted Hamilton's potential and signed him to a contract as part of McLaren's driver development programme. Hamilton continued racing go-karts until 2001, by which time he was European Champion and, in a quirk of fate, his teammate in his last two years of karting was future Mercedes teammate Nico Rosberg.

Hamilton was then to progress to Formula Renault racing where he finished third in his first full season as a 16 year old before winning the Championship in his second season at just 17.

This earned him a drive in the Formula 3 Championship where, after a year to bed-in, he would then have a fifth place finish in the Championship including his first race win at Formula 3 level.

This was just a preview of what was to come though, as the following year Hamilton would dominate - winning 15 out of 20 races to be crowned Champion. A move to Formula 1 feeder championship GP2 came in 2006 and Hamilton would go on to win the championship in his only season at this level.

Hamilton's success at all levels meant a move to Formula 1 was almost guaranteed and this was to come in 2007 when, at just 22 years old, Hamilton lined up at the Australian Grand Prix. Hamilton showed his potential immediately as he finished third in his first Grand Prix. In fact, Hamilton would go on to finish on top of the podium in all of his first nine races, including his first-ever Grand Prix victory in Canada which he quickly followed up by winning the very next Grand Prix in the USA. Hamilton would go on to agonisingly finish second in the championship in his debut season, just one point behind eventual winner Kimi Räikkonen.

The very next year Hamilton would go from agony to ecstasy though, as he was crowned World Champion in dramatic scenes in the final race of the season in Brazil. Hamilton was to go into the race as the championship leader and just needed a fifth place finish to guarantee his maiden title. In a race that featured rain showers, Hamilton was sitting in sixth place entering the final lap and it looked like he was going to miss out on the championship once again, however Hamilton was to race the lap of his life passing Timo Glock on the very last corner to clinch the title and become the youngest-ever World Champion.

The next few years were not to be as kind to Hamilton as his McLaren car struggled to keep pace with the dominant Red Bull car.

Hamilton was to make the move to the newly-formed Mercedes team to begin the 2013 season and his new car showed promise in its first season as Hamilton finished fourth in the championship standings. Having now gained the experience required, the Mercedes team would go on to dominate the F1 scene as Hamilton would add titles number two and three to his resume in 2014 and 2015. With many years ahead of him, and a competitive car under him, few would be surprised if Hamilton was to add more to this before he decides to call time on his racing career.

If You're Old Enough, You're Good Enough:
Young Guns of Formula One

While it could be said that there is a certain level of experience that is required to become a Formula One driver, that is not to say that there are not teams out there that are willing to give youth a chance.

IN FACT, THE HISTORY OF FORMULA ONE is littered with tales of drivers still in their teens battling it out with the elder statesmen on the grid in the hunt for the chequered flag.

With all teams on the lookout for the next great World Champion it is becoming more and more common

to see riders still in, or barely out of, their teens taking to the track. The youngest-ever to start a race was current Red Bull driver Max Verstappen, who remarkably was only 17 years and 166 days old when he made his debut in the 2015 Australian Grand Prix. Unbelievably there were certain races Verstappen competed in during the season where he was not old enough to hold a driving licence in that country, but was racing an F1 car at over 200 miles an hour mixing with the likes of Lewis Hamilton and Sebastian Vettel. Verstappen has still not turned 21 years old (he turned 20 in September 2017) yet is now a veteran of over 50 Grands Prix as he goes in search of becoming the youngest ever Champion in the sports history.

Come to think of it, having mentioned Hamilton and Vettel, these were two drivers who started at a very young age as well. Hamilton was the youngest-ever man to lead the World Championship in his debut season in 2007 and Vettel still holds the record as the Youngest World Champion ever, as he was 23 years and 134 days old when he clinched his first World Championship back in 2010.

The sport is encouraging younger drivers to take to the grid as the hope that youthful exuberance will lead to titles taking hold. Going into the 2017 season there were three drivers in the field who had all made their debuts at 20 years or younger and were still under 21

years old. They were Verstappen, Williams Lance Stroll and Esteban Ocon of Force India. A further

two riders, who would now be classed as more experienced, also made their debut while still in their teens; these being multiple World Champion Fernando Alonso and Toro Rosso man Daniel Kyvat.

That is not to say that this is a totally new phenomenon in the sport though, as you can go all the way back to 1961 to find the first ever driver under the age of 20 to compete in a F1 Grand Prix. That was Mexican Ricardo Rodriguez who lined up in the Italian Grand Prix at the tender age of 19 years and 208 days. Unfortunately for Rodríguez this was not to be the start of a long and trophy laden career as he retired from that particular race and would feature in only four others over the course of that season and the next.

The next man to attempt the feat was New Zealand's Chris Amon who made his debut in the 1963 Belgian Grand Prix at the age of 19 years and 324 days. While never World Champion, this was to be the start of a long and varied career in F1 which led to 108 races over 13 years in what was a smaller calendar.

So while this has been going on for years what has led to the uptick in younger drivers taking to the grid in recent years? Sauber driver Marcus Ericsson believes it is a current fad and it may change as time passes saying, "I can see the younger guys coming in, but still, for some reason, at the moment in Formula 1 there's a bit of a hype around that everyone needs to be so young"

However, many believe the trend is here to stay and with almost every team now having a driver development programme scouting the globe for the hottest young talent, the message has never been clearer: if you are old enough, you are good enough!

ROAD TO STARDOM
How to Become a Formula One Driver

SO WHO HASN'T DREAMT of emulating their heroes and racing from the pole position to take the chequered flag in front of thousands of adoring fans at Silverstone or Monaco? But how exactly do Formula 1 drivers get to that stage and what can you do to drive in their tracks?

WELL FOR ALMOST ALL FORMULA ONE DRIVERS their careers started in the junior ranks of the karting circuits. The major advantage of this is there are often no age restrictions like there is with car racing and some F1 drivers such as Lance Stroll started racing karts as young as five years old.

Don't worry if you are a little bit older than five years old as you read this, as there are many examples of others who didn't start racing until a lot later, such as former World Champion Kimi Räikkönen who was

almost a teenager before he raced his first lap, and there are others who did not start till they were well into their teens.

If you show a glimpse of talent in the karting ranks and start piling up the trophies then there is a good chance that you will be noticed by one of the current rider development programmes that Formula 1 teams have in order for them to find the next World Champion to race in their colours. This has helped stars such as Lewis Hamilton, who was snapped up by

McLaren as a 13 year old after telling then-team manager Ron Dennis that he would one day race for him when getting his autograph at the age of nine.

These driver development schools will often sponsor drivers or give them rides in other classes of racing. One of the most popular of these is Formula Renault which is widely regarded as the best introduction to single seat racing where drivers can learn advanced race craft in a competitive environment.

Many of the current Formula 1 field have been Formula Renault Champions in the past, including Kimi Räikkönen who jumped straight from this discipline to Formula 1 and Lewis Hamilton who used it as a stepping stone on his way to stardom.

Once a driver has mastered a series such as Formula Renault it is normally onto to one of the Formula 1 feeder series such as Formula 3, World Series by Renault or Formula 2.

Formula 3 is seen as where amateurs and professionals part ways, as anyone who is serious about becoming a F1 star has to make their mark at this level and, unlike the F1 calendar which sees races in numerous different countries around the world, F3 tends to be more regionalised with individual series taking place in the likes of Japan, Australia, Brazil and the UK, although there are a few that span Europe or South America for the more advanced drivers.

From Formula 3 it is normally onto Formula 2. F2, as it is normally known, follows the F1 calendar as one of the support races before the F1 Grand Prix.

F2 is seen as the pinnacle of single seat racing outside of Formula 1 and no less than seven of the current F1 field made the jump there from F2 including Hamilton, Nico Hülkenberg, Marcus Ericsson and Romain Grosjean.

If a driver is not deemed good enough to make the jump straight from one of these disciplines of racing straight to F1 then there is one more chance for him to impress. This is by getting what is known as a test drive for a F1 team.

This is very much as it sounds, whereby a driver will help the team with testing new engines and equipment on the track in the hope that they can do this quicker than current members of a team and impress enough to be awarded a seat in the team for real. Many of the current crop of F1 stars have gone down this route and it is a tried and tested method of success.

So there you have it; a guide as to how you can live out your dreams and take that chequered flag in Formula 1 – see you on top of the podium!

Vettel
on the Hunt

SEBASTIAN
VETTEL

Factfile

Date of Birth: 3 July 1987

Born: Heppenheim, Germany

Best-Ever Championship Finish: World Champion 2010, 2011, 2012, 2013

Current Team: Ferrari

THE MOST-DECORATED DRIVER currently lining up at the grid in Formula 1 is German superstar Sebastian Vettel. Vettel is a four-time World Champion; remarkably these came in four consecutive years in 2010, 2011, 2012 and 2013. The Ferrari racer currently holds a host of records including most points in a season; most wins in a season; most podiums in a season; most pole positions in a season and the youngest-ever man to win a World Championship and, as Vettel is still only 30 years, old there is no doubt that many more championship chases are ahead.

Vettel has been nicknamed 'Il Dito' by his Ferrari mechanics. This translates as 'the finger' and relates to the signature celebration that Vettel has when winning races. Born and raised in western Germany, growing up Vettel classed his heroes as Formula 1 legend Michael Schumacher; basketball star Michael Jordan and singer Michael Jackson, although it has to be said that Schumacher is the one he has emulated the most.

Racing Career

Vettel is one of the most experienced riders on the grid in any F1 race having now been a regular since 2006 and a veteran of almost 200 races.

Prior to his glittering F1 career, Vettel started his racing career by entering his first kart series at the age of eight however he had been driving karts since the age of three. At the age of 16 he moved onto open wheel racing and the German Formula BMW series which he promptly won. Vettel then moved onto the Formula 3 series. Two seasons at this level saw a still only 18 years old Vettel finish fifth and second in the standings and Formula 1 teams began to take notice.

A test drive for the Williams team was to follow before Sauber decided they had seen enough and gave him a seat in their

Just one year later though and a lack of reliability meant that Vettel could not challenge for his fifth World Championship and, with his relationship with Red Bull worsening, it was announced that he would be moving to perhaps the most famous F1 team of all - Ferrari. Unfortunately for Vettel his move to Ferrari has coincided with Mercedes dominance of the sport

team. At the time Vettel was the youngest-ever to compete in a F1 Grand Prix when making his debut at the 2007 USA Grand Prix, where he finished in the points in eighth place. This first drive alerted many other F1 teams to the undoubted potential of a still only 19 year old Vettel and first to the fore were the Red Bull team, who gave him a place in their second team Toro Rosso to start the 2008 season.

Unfortunately for Vettel his Toro Rosso car was one of the slowest on the grid so a season of frustrations lay ahead; this was not due to Vettel's lack of talent though and this was there for all to see when he almost claimed his first podium in wet conditions in the Japanese Grand Prix. 2008 saw the Toro Rosso car improve and Vettel continue to impress; including his first career win in F1 when he took the chequered flag in the Italian Grand Prix. This result, among others, helped Vettel to eighth place in the championship and a move to the senior Red Bull team to start the 2009 season.

A period of dominance which the sport has almost never seen before was to follow as the driving instincts of Vettel, coupled with the technological brilliance of the Red Bull car, meant Vettel was almost unstoppable in claiming four World Championships in the next five years. The best of these titles was in 2013 when Vettel remarkably won 13 of the 19 races (and this could have been 14 but for mechanical problems causing a retirement when leading the British Grand Prix). The records Vettel set that season for most wins and most points still stand and this was as dominant a season as the sport has ever seen.

and so far Vettel has not finished any better than third since joining the team. However, with Ferrari the most celebrated of all the teams and Vettel still young and hungry for title number five, there is still plenty of time for this to change.

The British Grand Prix

While there are many who will argue that Monaco is the most famous of Grands Prix (or each individual nationality may argue that the race held in their country is the cream of the crop!) in most people's eyes the most famous Grand Prix of them all is our very own British Grand Prix.

FIRST HELD ALL THE WAY BACK IN 1926 as a standalone race - Formula 1 did not become a Championship series until 1950 - the British Grand Prix is the longest

running continuous race in Formula 1. First run at the Brooklands track, which was the first custom-built race course in the UK, the race made the move to its spiritual home of Silverstone in 1948 and it is still held there to this day. In fact, the first ever Formula 1 Grand Prix was held there all the way back in 1950.

Silverstone is so named after the local village that borders the race track and lies on the border of the English counties of

Northamptonshire and Buckinghamshire. The circuit is built on an old RAF base and the runways can still be seen on the outskirts of the track to this day. The current F1 race track is 3.667 miles long and the current lap record is 1 minute 30.6 seconds, held by Lewis Hamilton.

The history of the track is varied and, as previously mentioned, the land was first used as an RAF base in the Second World War. After the end of hostilities a bunch of local racing enthusiasts decided to use the now deserted land as a race track and this led to the Royal Automobile Club taking on the land lease and making it an official race track for the first time.

The track remained largely the same for 40 years with just a few minor adjustments, mostly for safety, made during this time. The track was to undergo a major change during 1990-1991 to make it more technical and tricky for riders and further changes were made in 1994 to improve safety even more.

The most recent changes were made in 2011 and since then the track has remained unchanged.

How a Formula One Car Races the Track

The start of the track was relocated to between Club Corner and Abbey Corner. The first corner is almost flat out, the right-hander of Abbey leads immediately into the left-hander of Farm before cars brake heavily into the second gear, right-handed turn three; Village Corner.

The even slower left-hander of the Loop comes immediately after, and leads into the flat-out left-hander of Aintree, before cars head down the DRS zone of the Wellington Straight, designed in 2010 to promote overtaking at the track.

Turn 6, the left-hander of Brooklands, is taken by drivers in second gear and leads immediately into Luffield, another second gear curve; a right-hand hairpin.

The right-handed kink of Woodcote leads cars down the old pit straight, before the difficult sixth-gear right-hander of Copse, with a minimum speed of 175 mph in the dry for Formula 1 cars.

Then comes the challenging complex of Maggotts, Becketts and Chapel - a left-right-left-right-left complex with a minimum speed of 130 mph, it leads cars down the 770 metre Hangar Straight with the fifth-gear right-hander of Stowe at the end.

The 15th turn of the track, Stowe, has a minimum speed of 125 mph and precedes a short straight, named Vale, which leads cars downhill towards the Club complex.

Heavy braking is required for the left-hander of turn 16, and under steer can be an issue for the next right-handers of turns 17 and 18, as cars tentatively accelerate round to the start-finish straight. Stick to that formula and you will be right up there chasing track record holder, and five-time winner, Lewis Hamilton all the way to the chequered flag.

With almost 70 years of history, the British Grand Prix has seen some of the most memorable moments in Formula 1 history. Let's take a look back at some…

Start Line Crash, 1973

The 1973 British Grand Prix saw one of the biggest crashes in the history of the sport. Young South African Jody Scheckter crashed into the pit wall

coming out of the last corner. His car then bounced back into the centre of the track leaving the drivers behind him with nowhere to go. A total of 11 cars had to retire form the race after the incident. Thankfully, in an era where safety was not as prevalent as it is today, everyone managed to walk away from the incident.

Fan Protest, 2003

While won by Rubens Barrichello, the 2003 race is remembered for one reason only and that is the actions of one man. Priest Cornelius Horan ran onto the track while the race was in full flow, running towards the cars while they were at full speed waving placards in protest. The quick thinking of a steward got

Horan of the track without incident although he was later jailed for his actions.

A Star is Born, 2008

Lewis Hamilton had made a tremendous start to his Formula 1 career, finishing second in the 2007 Championship, but the race that marked him out as the star he has become was undoubtedly the drive at

Silverstone in 2008. In horrendously wet conditions that almost led to the race being stopped, Hamilton was in complete control winning the race by more than a minute and lapping all bar three other drivers in the field.

High Five, 2017

Hamilton made it five wins in total and four in a row in 2017 in a race he completely dominated, setting a new lap record in the process as well. Hamilton joined Alain Prost and Jim Clark as the only drivers with five wins and Clark as the only with four on the bounce. Can he make it six wins in total and five in a row in 2018?

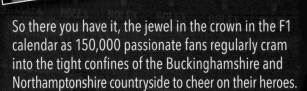

So there you have it, the jewel in the crown in the F1 calendar as 150,000 passionate fans regularly cram into the tight confines of the Buckinghamshire and Northamptonshire countryside to cheer on their heroes.

Finn it to Win it

VALTERRI BOTTAS

Factfile

Date of Birth: 28th August 1989

Born: Nastola, Finland

Best-Ever Championship Finish: 4th, 2014

Team: Mercedes

Racing Career

LOOKING TO MAINTAIN the recent Mercedes dominance of the Individual and Constructors' Championships is Finnish speedster Valterri Bottas.

Bottas was the recipient of the Mercedes seat that became available after Nico Rosberg's unexpected retirement and will be looking to make the most of this and carry on the form shown by Rosberg last season. Bottas was a latecomer to the Formula 1 field, making his debut in 2013 at the age of 24 - although he was a vastly experienced racer by that point, having competed in karting and the Formula 3 series with some success.

Like almost all the drivers in the field, Bottas' career started early on the karting circuit at the age of six with numerous titles coming his way in both his native Finland and all over Europe. Moving onto car racing at the age of 17 in the Formula Renault series, Bottas came third in his debut season before going on to dominate the next year, winning 17 of the 28 races on the way to the title. This brought Bottas to the attention of current Williams's technical director Toto Wolff and his boyhood hero, and former F1 World Champion, Mika Häkkinen. This saw Bottas make the jump to the F1 feeder series Formula 3 and GP3 and impress in both yet again.

Bottas finally made the step up to Formula 1, with his debut coming in the season-opening Australian Grand Prix in 2013. Racing in an uncompetitive Williams car, Bottas could only crack the top ten once in his debut season finishing the year with four championship points and a 17th place finish.

2014 was to be a whole lot better as Bottas used his experience of the circuits to markedly improve his results, with six podium finishes on the way to his best-ever World Championship finish of fourth place; this coinciding with Williams' change from a Renault to a Mercedes engine. This expertise of the Mercedes engine may well be what brought Bottas to the attention of the works Mercedes team that he now drives for and he will be looking to utilise this as he goes in search of his first World Championship.

The Iceman Cometh

KIMI RÄIKKÖNEN

Factfile

Date of Birth: 17th October 1979

Born: Espoo, Finland

Best-Ever Championship Finish: World Champion 2007

Team: Ferrari

Racing Career

ONE OF THE MOST INTERESTING CHARACTERS in the history of F1 is Ferrari's Kimi Räikkönen. 'The Iceman', as he is nicknamed, has had a chequered career that has seen him reach the heights of World Champion, but also saw him walk away from F1 to chase his dream to become World Rally Champion. Räikkönen his famous for his off-track behaviour having entered into such diverse competitions as snowmobile and powerboat racing, all while contracted to a F1 team. Räikkönen is also famous for his lack of interaction with the media but he justifies this by saying that all he wants to do his race… something he is very good at indeed.

Starting his career in what else but karting, Räikkönen was a relatively late entry to this discipline being as he was 11 before he got behind the wheel. He made up for this by wining multiple championships before moving to the UK to start his car racing career in Formula Renault at the age of 21. A dominate championship win in his first season saw many F1 teams take note and Kimi was quickly snapped up to ride for the Sauber team. This was a controversial decision as Räikkönen was viewed as massively inexperienced, having only had 23 races in a single seat car to this stage, but Peter Sauber (the owner of the team) vouched for Räikkönen and his licence was granted; this decision was immediately deemed correct as Räikkönen raced to a sixth place finish in his first-ever Grand Prix and backed this up by finishing a respectable tenth place in the Championship. Räikkönen's performance gained the attention of the McLaren team and a move to them to start the 2002 season was competed. This allowed the Finn to build on his debut season as he recorded four podium finishes on the way to a sixth place finish in the Championship. The following year was to see a maiden victory as Kimi won the second race of the season of the season in Malaysia. This was to be a springboard for a season in which Räikkönen raced to a second place finish in the Championship.

This form could not be duplicated in 2004 as car issues which saw five retirements in the first seven races meant his championship challenge was over before it had really begun. A further two title-less years were to follow at McLaren before Räikkönen made the shock move to bitter rivals Ferrari to start the 2007 season.

This turned out to be the best decision of Kimi's career as he became the first-ever man to win the World Championship in his first season with the Black Horse in the closest Championship ever. Both Lewis Hamilton and Fernando Alonso finished just one point behind Räikkönen, with Räikkönen taking victory in the last race with Alonso held back to third and Hamilton, who had been heavy favourite to take the title, slipping back to seventh due to a gearbox problem.

This was to be the one and only time Kimi would clinch the title as Red Bull were to dominate the sport for the next few years. This led to Kimi stepping away from Formula 1 to complete his childhood dream of competing in the World Rally Championship, but the allure of F1 was to prove too great and Räikkönen was back on the grid to start the 2012 season. Räikkönen has not been able to recapture the form that saw him lift the Championship ten years ago, but with the Ferrari car improving all the time no one would be shocked if The Iceman had one last championship burst in him.

The Big Formula One Quiz

30 Questions to test your knowledge on!

Award yourself one point for each correct answer. Some carry a bonus point for difficulty... plus a fiendishly difficult set of questions to finish!

1. Which driver has won the most F1 World Championships ever?

2. Which driver is nicknamed 'The Iceman'?

3. Who is the youngest-ever man to win the F1 World Championship?

4. How many British World Champions has there been in F1 history?

5. Name the different teams that Lewis Hamilton has driven for? [2pts]

6. Who were Red Bull's drivers for the 2017 season? [2pts]

7. Where is the Italian Grand Prix held?

8. Who won the 2016 F1 World Championship?

9. Which Constructor has the most Constructor Championships in the history of F1?

10. And how many times has that team won the Constructors Championship? [2pts]

11. Which Grand Prix traditionally starts the F1 Season?

12. Four former World Champions had team places at the start of the 2017 season. Can you name them?

13. Which Nationality is William's driver Lance Stroll?

14. How many different teams started the 2017 F1 season?

15. How many different race tracks have held the British Grand Prix? [2pts]

16. How many of the Formula 1 races take place on streets rather than race tracks?

17. Name them...? [2pts]

18. How many of the teams currently competing in F1 use a Ferrari engine?

19. Who won the first-ever Drivers Championship in 1950?

20. How many races did Sebastian Vettel win in 2013 (the year he set the record for most in a season)?

21. In what years did McLaren's Fernando Alonso win his World Championships?

22. Where does the USA Grand Prix take place?

23. What nationality is McLaren driver Stoffel Vandoorne?

24. Where does the Japanese Grand Prix take place?

25. Who is the youngest-ever driver to take place in a Grand Prix?

26. And who is the oldest? [2pts]

27. Who has started the most Grand Prix in the history of the sport? [2pts]

28. How many Grand Prix took place in 1950 (the sports first-ever year)? [2pts]

29. Two drivers have won the World Championship in only their second season. Can you name them? [2pts]

30. What is the top speed ever recorded in a F1 car and who recorded it? [2pts]

How did you do?

35-40 Points – World Champion

25-35 Points – Podium Finish

20-25 Points – In the Points Positions

10-20 – Developing Driver

0-10 – Back to Go Karting for you

29

Quiz answers on page 61

Globetrotters
Formula One:
A Worldwide Phenomenon

IT IS HARD to believe that when Formula 1 started all the way back in 1950 there were only seven races and six of these were in Europe, with the only one that was not being held in Indianapolis, USA.

Fast forward to 2017 and we have a 20 race calendar taking in all corners of the globe from Australia to the Middle East, Europe and the Americas.

The season traditionally opens in Australia and that was the case once again in 2017 as the Albert Park circuit in Melbourne hosts the event year on year. It's one of the most anticipated Grand Prix of the year as everyone looks forward to the start of the new season.

After the season opener in Australia F1 then moves onto China and the Shanghai international circuit, followed by Bahrain, which was the first-ever Grand Prix held in the Middle East when it was first run in 2004.

The Formula 1 circus then makes its way to Europe via Russia and a street race around the recently built Olympic park in Sochi. So, only four races in and already the globetrotting has taken the teams and drivers from Australia to Russia.

It's then a busy spell of races as Europe is predominantly home for the next few months. A mix of some of the most famous races on the circuit including the British Grand Prix, Monaco, Italian Grand Prix at Monza and Spanish Grand Prix in

Barcelona are mixed in with some lesser known races in places such as Azerbaijan and Austria.

After a summer in Europe it is back on their travels for all involved in Formula 1 as Asia is the next destination with Singapore, Malaysia and Japan all hosting a Grand Prix in quick succession.

It's then on to the Americas for the final leg of the season as the fans in the USA, Mexico and Brazil all get their chance to cheer on their favourites as the season reaches its climax.

A glittering event is held for the last Grand Prix of the season with the Abu Dhabi Grand Prix in the stunning surrounds of the Yas Marina Circuit. This is one of the most visually striking Grand Prix on the circuit, with the race starting in the daylight before night falls and the end of the race comes under the floodlights, as the chance of seeing a driver crowned F1 Champion is the ultimate for all fans in attendance.

So there you have it - should you want to follow F1 around the globe, you need to get yourself a nice fresh passport (and a healthy bank balance) as you will take in different cultures, cuisines, and conditions,

all of
which add
to the ultimate
challenge that is
being a Formula 1 driver.

So how do the teams manage it?
Well, while in Europe (where
all the teams are based)
the teams handle their own
transport in large team trucks
that crisscross the Continent from
the team's bases to circuit after circuit.

However for races in other parts of the world, the cars and all other parts, materials and equipment from the team's motor homes and garages are sent around the world in six jumbo jets, and in hundreds of sea crates sometimes weeks in advance of the race.

Formula 1 truly is a globetrotting sport and it may be the only one that takes in as many corners of the world on such a regular basis. Do you think you could manage to cope with the constant travelling?

1 Australian Grand Prix – 26 March	**11 Hungarian Grand Prix – 30 July**
Melbourne Grand Prix Circuit, Melbourne	Hungaroring, Budapest
2 Chinese Grand Prix – 9 April	**12 Belgian Grand Prix – 27 August**
Shanghai International Circuit, Shanghai	Circuit de Spa-Francorchamps, Stavelot
3 Bahrain Grand Prix – 16 April	**13 Italian Grand Prix – 3 September**
Bahrain International Circuit, Sakhir	Autodromo Nazionale Monza, Monza
4 Russian Grand Prix – 30 April	**14 Singapore Grand Prix – 17 September**
Sochi Autodrom, Sochi	Marina Bay Street Circuit, Singapore
5 Spanish Grand Prix – 14 May	**15 Malaysian Grand Prix – 1 October**
Circuit de Barcelona-Catalunya, Barcelona	Sepang International Circuit, Kuala Lumpur
6 Monaco Grand Prix – 28 May	**16 Japanese Grand Prix – 8 October**
Circuit de Monaco, Monte Carlo	Suzuka International Race Course, Suzuka
7 Canadian Grand Prix – 11 June	**17 United States Grand Prix – 22 October**
Circuit Gilles Villeneuve, Montreal	Circuit of the Americas, Austin, Texas
8 Azerbaijan Grand Prix – 25 June	**18 Mexican Grand Prix – 29 October**
Baku City Circuit, Baku	Autódromo Hermanos Rodríguez, Mexico City
9 Austrian Grand Prix – 9 July	**19 Brazilian Grand Prix – 12 November**
Red Bull Ring, Spielberg	Autódromo José Carlos Pace, São Paulo
10 British Grand Prix – 16 July	**20 Abu Dhabi Grand Prix – 26 November**
Silverstone Circuit, Silverstone	Yas Marina Circuit, Abu Dhabi

Wordsearch

Find the words in the grid.

Words can go horizontally, vertically and
diagonally in all eight directions.

H	R	P	K	F	G	G	N	X	R	J	L	D
B	O	T	T	A	S	V	P	L	D	Z	E	S
K	Y	S	O	S	N	O	L	A	B	R	T	N
M	L	B	E	H	K	Z	R	W	R	R	T	E
M	R	V	C	D	K	M	I	Q	O	M	E	P
T	C	N	T	V	E	R	G	L	F	N	V	P
N	X	L	B	M	A	C	L	L	O	M	B	A
P	G	B	A	R	P	K	R	T	N	A	R	T
N	Q	G	R	R	X	E	L	E	T	S	X	S
M	P	E	J	Q	E	I	R	P	M	S	Z	R
B	F	X	Z	P	M	N	M	E	W	A	T	E
J	L	G	D	A	G	Q	K	Z	Z	T	C	V
G	Z	R	H	R	E	N	A	U	L	T	L	W

Alonso	Mercedes
Bottas	Perez
Ferrari	Renault
Hamilton	Stroll
Massa	Verstappen
McLaren	Vettel

Wordsearch answers on page 60

Crossword

ACROSS

1 Nationality of Ferrari's Kimi Räikkönen (7)

3 David; Scottish driver who raced in 246 Grand Prix between 1994 and 2008 (9)

5 Sebastian; driver known as 'Il Dito' (6)

6 Traditional home of the British Grand Prix

9 Venue for 2017 Chinese Grand Prix (8)

15 Romain; Haas Ferrari driver (8)

16 Brazilian; three-time Championship winner (6,5)

17 Graham and Damon; father and son who were both World Champions (4)

18 Team name: Force _____ (5) (6)

19 Venue of final Grand Prix of 2017 season (3,5)

DOWN

2 Nico; Renault driver in 2017 (10)

3 Jim; British-born former World Champion, ranked by many as the best British driver of all time (5)

4 Fernando; Spanish-born McLaren driver (6)

7 Marcus; Swedish-born; 2017 Sauber driver (8)

8 Venue of the Hungarian Grand Prix (11)

10 2016 Constructors' Champion (7)

11 Antonio; Sauber driver for 2017 (10)

12 Circuit that has the famous Marina section (6)

13 Jenson; last British driver to win a World Championship before Lewis Hamilton (6)

14 Team known as 'the Scuderia' (7)

35

Crossword answers on page 60

Red Bull
Team

Red Bull
Team

MAX
VERSTAPPEN

DANIEL
RICCIARDO

Factfile

Date of Birth: 30th September 1997
Born: Hasselt, Belgium
Best-Ever Championship Finish: 5th, 2016
Team: Red Bull

Factfile

Date of Birth: 1st July 1989
Born: Perth, Australia
Best-Ever Championship Finish: 3rd, 2014 & 2016
Team: Red Bull

Racing Career

RED BULL RACING SHOCKED THE FORMULA ONE WORLD when they gave a 17 year old Max Verstappen a seat in their secondary team - Toro Rosso - to start the 2015 season. Up to this point Verstappen had only had one season in single seater racing but the Red Bull bosses saw something in Verstappen and he was to quickly repay this faith as he raced admirably to record 49 points and a 12th place finish in the Championship during his maiden season.

Verstappen is another who was almost always destined to become a F1 driver; his father was renowned racer Jos Verstappen who competed in no less than 106 Grands Prix and his mother Sophie Kumpen was a champion kart racer. Like almost all of your favourite F1 stars, Max started his career in karting at a young age and by nine years old was Dutch and Belgian champion. Verstappen's prodigious talent meant that by age 15 he was to be karting World Champion and a step-up to car racing was inevitable.

Formula 3 was to be the destination for Verstappen and, even though he was the youngest rider in the field, he was to finish third in his one and only season at this level, before the shock move to Toro Rosso was to follow. Verstappen is seen by many as a World Champion of the future and this belief was reinforced with some unbelievable drives in the 2016 season, in which the young Belgian finished fifth in the standings. This included his first-ever race win in a Formula 1 Grand Prix in Spain having started the race from fourth on the grid.

Racing Career

AUSSIE-BORN RACER DANIEL RICCIARDO is another who is on the hunt for his first-ever Formula 1 Championship, now being an experienced racer of more than 120 Grands Prix dating back to his debut in 2011.

Ricciardo, like current team mate Max Verstappen, was a product of the Red Bull Driver Development Program. Nicknamed the Honey Badger due to his fearlessness and ruthlessness on the track, Ricciardo was brought up on the outskirts of Perth in Western Australia to Italian parents. His father was a keen amateur race driver and this is where Daniel caught the racing bug from. A glittering karting career led to a race in the Western Australia Formula Ford Championship and, despite an uncompetitive car, his racing instincts were there for all to see.

Ricciardo then moved to Europe where successful Formula Renault and Formula 3 campaigns led him to the attention of the Red Bull team who looked to see what he could do in a F1 car by paying for him to compete in the second half of the 2011 season for the Hispania Racing team. Ricciardo did enough to impress Red Bull and a move to their second team Toro Rosso was in place for the start of the 2012 season. Two seasons at Toro Rosso followed before a promotion to the full Red Bull team was to come. In his debut season with Red Bull in 2014 Ricciardo raced to his first-ever race win in the Canadian Grand Prix. He backed this up with a further two wins that season en route to a third place finish in the Championship. This still ranks as his best-ever season for race wins, although his best-ever points tally was to come in the 2016 season, where he raced to seven podium finishes as he equalled his third place finish from 2014.

Williams Mercedes Team

FELIPE MASSA

Factfile

Date of Birth: 25th April 1981
Born: São Paulo, Brazil
Best-Ever Championship Finish: 2nd, 2008
Team: Williams Mercedes

Racing Career

ONE OF THE MOST EXPERIENCED DRIVERS ON THE GRID is Brazilian racer Felipe Massa. Massa has been a fixture in Formula 1 since way back in 2002 and, despite announcing he was to retire at the end of the 2016 season, Massa had a change of heart and lined up once again for the 2017 season.

Born in São Paulo, Massa cut his teeth racing in karting before moving to Europe as a 19 year old in 2000. Two years racing Formula Renault and Formula 3000 followed before his first drive in F1 with Sauber in 2002. The Sauber car was not competitive enough for Massa to challenge at the top end of the grid, however there were flashes of what was to come and in 2006 the Ferrari team decided to partner Massa with all-time great Michael Schumacher. This allowed Massa to showcase his undoubted talent and his first career race win was to come at the Turkish Grand Prix.

Massa then completed a lifetime ambition when he won his home Grand Prix in front of a large and passionate support, taking the chequered flag in the last race of the season confirming his third place finish in the Championship with the win. Massa would go one better than this in his finest-ever championship season in 2008, although Massa may see this as a chance for a World Championship missed, as he lost out to Lewis Hamilton by one solitary point after Hamilton passed Timo Glock on the last lap of the last race to snatch the Championship from Massa's hand.

Massa has never been able to replicate his form of that season and, as time ticks down on his F1 career, it may be that he never will.

Williams Mercedes Team

LANCE STROLL

Factfile

Date of Birth: 29th October 1998
Born: Montreal, Canada
Best-Ever Championship Finish: N/A [2017 was his first season]
Team: Williams Mercedes

Racing Career

WILLIAMS MADE MONTREAL-BORN LANCE STROLL one of the youngest drivers in F1 history when they handed him a seat for the 2017 Championship just a few months after his 18th birthday.

Raised in Canada, Lance was introduced to Motorsport when his father Lawrence, a keen amateur racer himself, bought his son a go-kart at the tender age of five. This may well turn out to be the best purchase of his father's life as Lance looks to make a name for himself in F1.

Stroll has been a Champion at every level he has raced at during his young career, having lifted the Italian Formula 4 Championship and European F3 Championship firstly as a development driver for Ferrari before Williams signed the youngster to a contract and offered him the seat for 2017.

It will be interesting to see how Stroll's career progresses but, if he takes to F1 the same way he did to any of the previous disciplines he has been involved in, then the man tipped by many to be a future World Champion may come good on this.

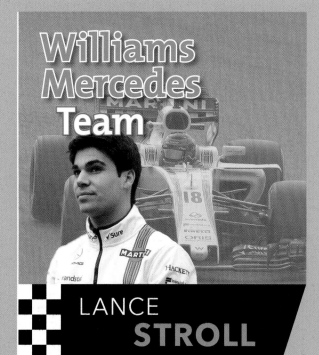

BEST
of the
BEST

MICHAEL
SHUMACHER

Schumacher was not afraid to mix it up either and was involved in several incidents, not least in 1994 when he clashed with Damon Hill; stopping the Englishman from winning his first-ever title at the time.

Schumacher retired from the sport in 2006 but was not away for long. The urge to compete returned and he was back in 2010. Unfortunately, this second spell in the sport was not as lucrative as the first, however this has not tarnished what was an unbelievable career and many view Schumacher as the best-ever with feats that will never be matched.

Factfile

Date of Birth: 3 January 1969

Born: Hurth, Germany

Years in Formula One: 1991–2006 & 2010–2012

World Championships: 7 (1994, 1995, 2000, 2001, 2002, 2003, & 2004)

WHILE MANY CURRENT FANS will argue that their favourites such as Sebastian Vettel, Lewis Hamilton or Fernando Alonso are the best drivers, let's have a look at some of the past stars who could lay claim to the title as Best-Ever in the history of Formula 1.

GERMAN SUPERSTAR MICHAEL SCHUMACHER was the epitome of efficiency and consistency during his long and illustrious career. Schumacher still holds numerous records including Most World Championships; Most Race Wins; Most Podiums and Most Pole Positions, among many others. Schumacher also showed he could do it in different cars, winning titles with both the Benetton and Ferrari teams.

AYRTON
SENNA

This led to an outpouring of grief in his native Brazil that has never been matched and Senna is still a hero for millions.

Senna was the master of difficult conditions and some of his drives in atrocious conditions had to be seen to be believed. His rivalry with Alain Prost made Formula 1 one of the most popular sports in the world in the 1980s and this has been well documented in many films and books.

Factfile

Date of Birth: 21st March 1960

Born: São Paulo, Brazil

Years in Formula One: 1984–1994

World Championships: 3 (1988, 1990 & 1991)

The legacy of Senna lives on through a charitable foundation set up in his name by his sister which has raised and donated over £100million, with the majority of this going to help needy children in his homeland of Brazil.

Despite his career being curt short, Senna still holds numerous records including Most Pole Positions in a row and the Most-Ever Wins leading the entire Grand Prix.

Senna was a true legend on and off the track and that is why many argue he is the greatest ever bar none.

BRAZILIAN BORN RACER AYRTON SENNA is one of the most loved drivers in the history of the sport. Senna was nicknamed 'Beco' which translates as 'alley' by his parents as a seven year old and this was to be a very apt nickname for Senna, who could be a fearsome competitor on the track, but off the track had a love for life that almost all found magnetic. Senna was also at the fore of driver safety and pushed through many improvements in this field in his time. Although his three Championships do not place him towards the top of the All-Time lists, many feel this would have been more but for his untimely death in a crash in the 1994 San Marino Grand Prix.

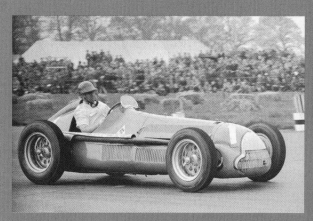

JUAN MANUEL FANGIO

Factfile

Date of Birth: 24th June 1911
Born: Balcarce, Argentina
Years in Formula One: 1950–1958
World Championships: 5 (1951, 1954, 1955, 1956, 1957)

THE FIRST-EVER SUPERSTAR OF FORMULA ONE was Argentinean Juan Manuel Fangio, who dominated the formative years of the sport taking home five of the first eight World Championships in the 1950s.

Nicknamed El Maestro (The Master), Fangio was a master of track craft, as proven by the fact that his five World Championships came with four different teams. While there were not the number of races in the early days of the sport to match the number of wins the likes of Michael Schumacher has, Fangio's greatness can be seen in the records he holds to this day - these being the Highest Percentage of Race Wins; Highest Percentage of Pole Positions and Highest Percentage of Front Row Starts. This shows just how dominant Fangio was in his time as he won almost half the races he entered in his eight year F1 career.

A truly fearless competitor, Fangio raced in an era where accidents were common and drivers generally had a short career. However his skill and vision allowed him to go on and clinch his five Championships with no one else close to competing at that level.

Fangio's legacy lives on and he is so revered in his native Argentina that a racing museum was named in his honour in 1986.

JIM
CLARK

Factfile

Date of Birth: 4th March 1936

Born: Kilmany, Scotland

Years in Formula One: 1960–1967

World Championships: 2 (1963, & 1965)

BRITAIN'S VERY OWN JIM CLARK completes the list of drivers. Many feel was he the greatest Formula 1 has ever seen. While his stats may not match up to some of his peers, it is the skill in which Clark could manipulate a car that lead many to say he is the Greatest Driver of All-Time.

Clark had a short career in Formula 1, only competing for seven years in the sport but what a glittering career it was with two World Championships and, at the time he retired, the Most Race Wins and Pole Positions ever by a driver in the sport.

One of the major reasons many say Clark was the best driver in the history of the sport was the versatility he had as a driver. Not only did Clark win two F1 World Championships, he was also crowned British Touring Car Champion in 1964 and won the Indianapolis 500 - perhaps the most famous race in the world at the time. Clark was also a keen racer of sports cars and finished third in the Le Mans 24 hour race in 1960.

It was this ability to race almost any vehicle that has many of his era saying Clark was the finest driver in the history of motor racing; not bad for the son of a farmer from Fife in Scotland.

Design of a Formula One Car

AS YOU SIT WATCHING your favourite driver race around the track at more than 200 miles per hour, have you ever wondered just how the car they are driving can do such speeds and just how are they built?

Well, it is all in the design and over the next few pages we will learn a little about just what goes into designing and building a F1 car.

Formula 1 cars are what are known as single seat, open cockpit, open wheel racing cars and it is fairly easy to understand why. They only have one seat and neither the cockpit where the driver sits or the wheels are enclosed or covered.

After that though, the design is where the magic happens as every inch of the car is designed with optimum speed in mind. Starting with the chassis, or body of the car which is made out of the lightest weight carbon fibre that can be found, in fact, the average Formula 1 car with driver in it weighs no more than an average size bull or a large horse.

As the car is so light the engine is not as powerful as you may imagine and amazingly, while turbo charged,

Teams will spend millions upon millions of pounds looking to shave even a tenth of a second of a lap time using aerodynamics as they know how much of a difference this can make on the track. Very often it is the difference between winning and losing a race, but how does a car generate this downforce?

a regular Formula 1 engine is only a 1.6 litres. There is a very good chance that the engine in the car sitting outside your house is actually more powerful, but of course the average car is around twice the weight of a Formula 1 car so it has more work to do.

Where the Formula 1 car truly separates itself from almost all other types of motorsport is in the use of aerodynamics to squeeze every last drop of speed out of the car. Aerodynamics has two main functions on an F1 car: the creation of downforce, to help push the car's tyres onto the track and improve cornering forces, and minimising the drag that gets caused by turbulence and acts to slow the car down. That is why you will hear commentators talk so much about these when watching a Grand Prix on a Sunday afternoon.

Well, you will have heard these same commentators talking about the 'wings' on a car and yes, just like a plane, F1 cars are fitted with their own types of wings; the only difference is these are designed to push the car into the ground instead of into the air like on a plane. Believe it or not the design of wings on F1 cars is so effective, and they create so much force, that a Formula 1 car could actually drive upside down on the ceiling of a building and it would not fall off!

Aerodynamics is thought of in the design of every single component of both the driver and car and not just the car itself. For example, did you know that the shape and material used for a drivers helmet, while concerned mostly with safety, also takes into account aerodynamics and the effect it can have on the speed of the car?!

As well as aerodynamics there are also certain tricks a driver has up his sleeve to help boost his speed during a race and many of these are controlled via the steering wheel. You may have seen a F1 steering wheel and wondered just what all those buttons are for. Every one of them has a use, from the obvious ones such as changing gears and changing the reading on the drivers display. However, the driver also has further tools at his disposal such as the ability to adjust the amount of air getting into the fuel; applying a limiter for safety car laps or when in the pits and, of course, the ability to call the radio and speak to his race mechanic or engineer. Believe it or not a steering wheel of an F1 car can cost over £50,000 to design and manufacture.

All of this leads to the performance that you see out on the track. A F1 car can go from 0-100 miles per hour and back to 0 in 5 seconds. Think about that for a second - count out 1, 2, 3, 4, 5… in that time a F1 car could get to 100 miles per hour and back! The highest-ever speed recorded on a race track in a F1 car was 234mph by Valtteri Bottas.

It's not just about straight line speed though; the level of downforce in a car means they can corner at higher speeds than almost any other race car in the world and due to the strain this can put on a drivers body, most F1 drivers have specific strength exercises just for their necks to cope with what is known as the g-force.

All of this comes at a cost with the average F1 car costing a whopping £7.5 million to design and build, The most expensive part of this being the engine which costs over £6 million and the bodywork over half a million pounds as well.

This is what it takes to be at the pinnacle of the most famous motor sport in the world and the cars truly are an unparalleled feat of modern engineering.

Force India Team

SERGIO PÉREZ

Factfile

Date of Birth: 26th January 1990
Born: Guadalajara, Mexico
Best-Ever Championship Finish: 7th, 2016
Team: Force India

Racing Career

MEXICAN SUPERSTAR SERGIO PÉREZ is now a veteran of the F1 circuit having been a regular on the grid since his debut at the Australian GP in 2011.

'Checo', as he is nicknamed, is much loved in his native Mexico due as much to his charity work as as to his racing exploits. Pérez formed the Checo Pérez Foundation in 2012, which supports children with cancer and who are orphaned. Pérez puts his celebrity and friendship with Mexican Football superstar Javier Hernández to good use to raise awareness of these issues.

On the track Pérez has improved in every season he has been in F1 with a seventh place finish in 2016 his finest finish to date. Now a veteran of over 130 Grands Prix, Pérez is still waiting on his first taste of the chequered flag with his best-ever race finish being second place; this being accomplished at both Malaysia and Italy in 2012. However, as his consistency has improved year-on-year, Pérez has become very accomplished and is a regular feature in the point positions. Whether Pérez has the ability to take the next step and challenge for a World Championship remains to be seen, but it will not be for a lack of trying and, aged only 27, time is still on Pérez's side.

Force India Team

ESTEBAN OCON

Factfile

Date of Birth: 17th September 1996
Born: Evreux, France
Best-Ever Championship Finish: 23rd, 2016
Team: Force India

Racing Career

HAILING FROM THE NORMANDY REGION of northern France, Esteban Ocon is looking to make his way on the F1 circuit. Another of the young generation of drivers that currently call Formula 1 home, Ocan is part of the Mercedes Benz driver development programme and, after he was brought in to race the last nine races for the now defunct Manor team in 2016, Mercedes decided to place him with their Force India team to see how he would progress in 2017.

Like many, Ocon started his career in karting as a ten year old. His talent was quickly noticed and as soon as he was old enough Ocon moved to the Formula Renault series, then followed this up by joining the Formula 3 and GP3 circuits. Ocon is also a distinguished Touring Car racer having completed in the top tier of this discipline of motor racing in the German DTM series before F1 became his sole focus.

Ocon was first contracted as a test driver for Renault in 2016 and impressed enough for Manor to give him his chance. Although he couldn't get himself into the points positions in what was the slowest car in the field, the experience will no doubt do Ocon good as he looks to make a career for himself in F1.

Toro Rosso Team

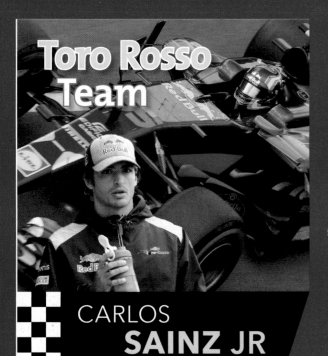

CARLOS
SAINZ JR

DANIIL
KYVAT

Factfile

Date of Birth: 1st September 1994
Born: São Madrid, Spain
Best-Ever Championship Finish: 12th, 2016
Team: Toro Rosso

Factfile

Date of Birth: 26th April 1994
Born: Ufa, Russia
Best-Ever Championship Finish: 7th, 2015
Team: Toro Rosso

Racing Career

ANOTHER YOUNG DRIVER hoping to make his way through the Red Bull driver development program is current Toro Rosso racer Carlos Sainz. Although only 22 at the start of the 2017 season, Sainz is already a veteran of two full seasons and is showing improvement year-on-year as he looks to follow in the steps of the likes of Max Verstappen and make the step from Toro Rosso to the full Red Bull team to challenge for a Championship.

Sainz is another with racing pedigree as he is the son of two times World Rally Champion Carlos Sainz Sr and it can be seen that racing flows through his blood in his style on the track.

Sainz followed the well-known path to Formula 1, starting his racing career in karting at a young age, winning the Junior Monaco Kart Cup in 2009 before moving on to Formula BMW in 2010.By this point he had been snapped up as part of the Red Bull junior racing team, finishing fourth in the Championship in his debut season.

This got Sainz a move to Formula 3 finishing ninth overall in the European Championship at only 18 years old at the time, marking him out as one to watch for the future. Spells in GP3 and Formula Renault were to follow before the big move to F1 and Toro Rosso to start the 2015 season.

His first season in F1 was to be tough as Sainz struggled for points; his best performance being a seventh place finish in the USA Grand Prix. Overall Sainz finished with 18 points and a 15th place finish in the Championship.

Better results were to follow as Sainz raced to 46 points and a 12th place finish in 2016 including three sixth place finishes, which is still his best to date.

Sainz continues to build year-on-year and many predict a top ten finish will be forthcoming and eventually a move to the full Red Team.

Racing Career

THE ONLY RUSSIAN to take his place on the grid is Toro Rosso racer Daniil Kyvat. Kyvat was born and raised in central Russia and, with no real family history in racing, it was a surprise when Daniil made his first steps in racing as an eight year old in local karting championships. His karting career was followed by the move to Formula BMW in 2010 where his talent shone through, leading to moves through the normal channels of Formula Renault and Formula 3, before his shock move to Formula 1 with Toro Rosso in 2014. Kyvat was only 19 years old when he took to the grid in the season opening Australian Grand Prix. His driving showed early promise with Kyvat finishing in the points in three of his first four races and finished his debut season 15th in the standings.

This was good enough for a promotion to the full Red Bull team for the 2015 season and Kyvat used this as a springboard to a seventh place Championship finish, with his best finish being a second place in the Hungarian Grand Prix.

Unfortunately for Kyvat 2016 was a tougher season with only 25 points accrued and it appears that Red Bull may be running out of patience with him. One final chance was presented with a move back to Toro Rosso for 2017, although it may be his final chance to stick as an F1 driver.

Rule Britannia!
Britain's Champions

BRITAIN has an illustrious career when it comes to Formula One with no fewer than ten different UK-born drivers claiming the world title. Add in to this multiple titles for some and a British driver has stood atop the podium at the end of the season no fewer than 16 times, which is the best for any one nation in the history of the sport. Germany comes second with 12, although these only came from three different drivers.

THE GOLDEN AGE for British drivers was in the 1960s and early 1970s when a British driver took the Championship in nine out of a possible 15 races. Let's take a closer look at some of those Champions…

The first-ever Brit to win the Formula 1 World Championship was Mike Hawthorn who raced his Ferrari to victory in 1958. Hawthorn was a veteran of the F1 circuit by this point having competed from 1952, however he had not made the breakthrough to win a Championship prior to this, mostly due to the excellence of Juan Fangio who dominated the sport in the years prior. Hawthorn won an exciting Championship by just one point from a fellow Brit Stirling

Moss in the last race of the season and, after being crowned Champion, decided he would never again reach these heights and retired from the sport.

It was to be four years before another Brit was to taste victory in the Championship but this was to start the Golden Age as the next four titles, and eight of the next 12, all went to British drivers. Next up after Hawthorn was Graham Hill in 1962. Hill

is widely regarded as one of the finest motor racers of all time as he is the only driver to claim what is known as the Motorsport Triple Crown - as well as being an F1 World Champion he also claimed victory in both the Indianapolis 500 and the Le Mans 24 Hour races, a feat that may never be repeated. Hill would also go on to claim a second F1 championship

six years later in 1968 and is still one of a shortlist of drivers who have won the Championship with two different manufacturers (BRM & Lotus).

Hill's victory in 1962 was followed up in 1963 by the first of two Championships for Scotsman Jim Clark. Clark dominated the season in 1963, winning the Championship in his Lotus Climax car with three races to spare in a season where there were only ten races

99 races and, always with a Ford engine in his car, raced to further world titles in both 1971 and 1973. This was also the year he decided to call time on his career.

in total. Clark repeated the same feat in 1965, again clinching the title in the same car.

1976 was to be another year of note for Brits in F1 as James Hunt won his one and only Championship. Hunt is perhaps more famous for his lifestyle off the track than for his exploits on it as he was a famous party-lover and enjoyed the jet set lifestyle that comes with being an F1 driver to the maximum. That is not to say he wasn't a fearsome competitor on track though. His title win in 1976 is the stuff of legend as he rode the race of his life to clinch the title by one point in the final laps of the Japanese Grand Prix, beating his great rival Niki Lauda.

Britain's domination continued in 1964 with John Surtees winning his one and only title. Surtees' claim to fame is that he is the only man to have ever won the World Motorbike Championship and F1 Championship, having won the bike championship four times. Surtees decided to try his hand at Formula 1 and ended up racing for 12 years, although 1964 was to be his one and only World Championship.

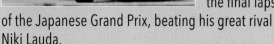

It was then a long 16-year wait until the next British World Champion was to emerge from these shores. This came in 1991 when Nigel Mansell became one of the most popular winners in the history of the

Clark and Hill claimed their second titles in the late 60s before, in 1969, another British star was born in the form of Jackie Stewart. Nicknamed 'The Flying Scotsman', Stewart is still one of the most recognised faces of the sport due to his commentating work on TV. He also had a spell as a team owner of the Stewart racing team in the late 1990s. Stewart is one of the most successful F1 drivers of all-time, racing to three Championships and two second places during his eight years in the sport. Stewart finished his career with 27 wins in

sport. Mansell had been in F1 for 11 years without winning a Championship and it was starting to look like time would run out. However, Mansell had one last great season in him and he won the Championship by a

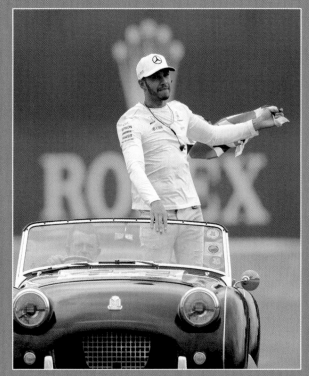

landslide, clinching the title with five races to go and running out victory by 52 points (this was a time when it was only ten points for a win).

This win was quickly followed up by another first time British winner in 1996 when Damon Hill took the title. You may recognise that surname, and yes, Damon was the son of former Champion Graham Hill, becoming the first-ever father-son duo to both win Championships (this has since been equalled by Keke and Nico Rosberg). Damon had had some famous run-ins with Michael Schumacher that had stopped him clinching a title before 1996, but that year everything was to come together and victory was clinched in the final Grand Prix of the season.

Unfortunately, 1996 was to signal the start of another long run before God Save the Queen was to be heard come season end, as Michael Schumacher and Fernando Alonso were to dominate for years. This came to an end in 2008 when Lewis Hamilton took the crown in dramatic fashion on the last corner of the last lap of the last race, after cruelly being denied the title in his first-ever season in the

sport in 2007. Hamilton has, of course, gone on to claim further Championships in both 2014 and 2015.

The last and final of the ten men born in Britain to have been crowned F1 Champion is Jenson Button,

who took the crown in 2009. Button was another who had spent years looking to hit the pinnacle of the sport and in the end finished his career with more than 300 races to his name, but his finest moment undoubtedly came at Brazilian Grand Prix in 2009. This was the second last race of that season and the one were Button clinched his title.

It is not just in the individual driver's Championship that Brits have prevailed as, amazingly, 33 times out

of 56 a team from Britain has won the Constructors' Championship.

*So there you have it, the ten men that have stood proudly atop the podium at the end of the season as the British flag is unfurled and the national anthem played crowning a lifetime of work. Who knows who will be the next one; **could it be you?***

Sauber Team

PASCAL WEHRLEIN

Factfile

Date of Birth: 18th October 1994
Born: Sigmaringen, Germany
Best-Ever Championship Finish: 19th, 2016
Team: Sauber

Racing Career

GERMAN DRIVER PASCAL WEHRLEIN is another who is trying to make it in the fast paced world of F1. Wehrlein has followed a slightly different path to F1, although it started in the same way as it has done for so many, in the junior karting ranks where he started competing as a nine year old. Formula 3 was the next step for the German, finishing second in his one and only year in the Euro series. This is where the story of Wehrlein's career moved in a different route as, rather than Formula 2 where so many drivers end up, he moved away from single seater racing to compete in the German Touring Car Championship. This is widely regarded as one of (if not the) toughest saloon car driving Championship in the world. This did not worry Wehrlein though, as at just 18 years old he made his debut.

A learning curve of a first season was built upon as he became the youngest ever driver to win a race in just his second season and in his third and final season he became the youngest-ever driver to win the Championship. This garnered the attention of F1 teams and in 2015 Wehrlein acted as a reserve and test driver for Mercedes. A switch to the Manor team came in 2016 as part of a mutual agreement with Mercedes. This debut year was a struggle as Wehrlein could only manage a solitary point in the Championship at the Austrian Grand Prix. So, another who may need to impress a little more should he want to stick in the cut-throat arena that is Formula 1.

Sauber Team

MARCUS ERICSSON

Factfile

Date of Birth: 2nd September 1990
Born: Kumla, Sweden
Best-Ever Championship Finish: 18th, 2015
Team: Sauber

Racing Career

AT 27 YEARS OLD, SWEDE MARCUS ERICSSON is now a veteran presence on the F1 grid having raced in over 60 F1 races so far. Ericsson, however, can perhaps be seen to be a little fortunate to still have his team place as his performances perhaps haven't merited his continued inclusion on the grid.

Ericsson is not used to struggling though as he had a glittering career in all categories he raced in before the switch to F1.

Ericsson started his career in 2007 winning the British Formula BMW Championship in his only season in the sport. A move to the British Formula 3 Championship where a solid campaign was to follow. This led to a move to Japan's Formula 3 series and another Championship win.

A move to GP2 followed, however this was to be the end of Ericsson's championship run as the best he could manage during three years in the sport was a sixth place finish. Despite this, the Caterham team decided that Ericsson had the capability of performing in the F1 and awarded him a seat in their team for that season. Ericsson could not bother the scorers though, with 11th being his best finish in the Monaco Grand Prix. The next season Ericsson moved to Sauber and his finest season was to follow with nine points and an 18th place finish. The last of these points came at the Italian Grand Prix and, as it stands, this was still the last time Ericsson made the Top Ten and many wonder, if this form doesn't improve, whether Ericsson will have a drive for much longer.

Renault Team

Renault Team

NICO HÜLKENBERG

Jolyon PALMER

Factfile

Date of Birth: 19th August 1987
Born: Emmerich am Rhein, Germany
Best-Ever Championship Finish: 12th, 2016
Team: Renault

Factfile

Date of Birth: 20th January 1991
Born: Horsham, United Kingdom
Best-Ever Championship Finish: 18th, 2016
Team: Renault

Racing Career

GERMAN NICO HÜLKENBERG is now one of the most experienced drivers on the grid as a veteran of over 120 races; his debut being all the way back in 2010. Hülkenberg has been a consistent performer although not one that has ever challenged for a world title. In fact Hülkenberg has never even managed a podium finish, with several fourth place finishes his best result. That is not to say that Hülkenberg can be taken lightly as a driver and his skill was shown when he was part of the winning team of the 2015 Le Mans 24 Hour race.

The son of a shipping company owner, Hülkenberg had a career as a freight agent lined up, should his racing career not have worked out, and he is fluent in German, Dutch and English. Hülkenberg started his racing career at ten years old in karting and won the German Junior Championship in his first year and the full German Championship in his second year, and his career was off and running.

By 2010 Hülkenberg was ready for F1 and a move to Williams. A promising first season saw Hülkenberg finish in the points seven times in his debut season.

This was not enough to keep Hülkenberg in the sport though, and a year as a test driver for Force India was to come. He impressed enough to earn a team place the following year and an 11th place finish followed. Hülkenberg's finest year was 2014 when he finished in the points in all bar four Grands Prix which was good enough for 96 points and a ninth place finish. Hülkenberg has shown flashes of his potential and, who knows, if he can break into a winning streak then he may go on a roll from there.

Racing Career

BRITISH RACER JOLYON PALMER is finding his way in F1 as he looks to carve out a career at the top level. The son of former F1 driver Jonathan Palmer, Jolyon is a relative late starter to racing starting his career at 14 and, also unusually, most of his early experiences were not in karts but in a series known as the T Car Championship. Palmer's performances impressed at this level so a move to Formula Audi followed; the series created by his father Jonathan.

 A serious quad bike crash almost cost Palmer his career at this stage but thankfully he was able to make a full recovery and continue his racing career. Palmer then moved onto the GP2 series improving year on year before clinching the title in 2014. This led to test drives for both Force India and Lotus in 2014 and 2015 where he routinely outpaced his teammates. These test performances earned Palmer his team place at Renault in 2016 but a tough season was to follow with just one solitary point to his name from a tenth place finish at the Malaysian Grand Prix. Renault stuck with Palmer for a second season in 2017 but it may be that, if performances don't improve, Palmer's F1 career could come to an end.

McLaren Team

FERNANDO ALONSO

Factfile

Date of Birth: 29th July 1981
Born: Oviedo, Spain
Best-Ever Championship Finish: World Champion 2005, 2006
Team: McLaren

Racing Career

THE FINAL of the four former World Champions currently still racing is Spanish legend Fernando Alonso. Alonso is also one of the elder statesmen on the grid being as he is now a veteran of more than 280 races, although perhaps his best days are behind him. It has now been ten full seasons since his last pair of World Championships when he completed back to back victories for the Renault team in 2005 and 2006.

Still a hero in his native Spain, Alonso also has three second places and a third to his name in the World Championship and stands amongst the all-time greats of the sport.

Alonso started his racing career at the age of three when he started racing on a kart his father had built for his older sister that she showed no interest in. By the time he was old enough to move on it was obvious what talent Alonso had.

Alonso had a short career in single seater racing prior to his first steps into Formula 1 just doing two years in the lower ranks before the jump to Formula 1 upon the Minardi team in 2001.

The Minardi team were not competitive though and Alonso struggled through the season not managing a single point. However, his talent had been spotted and a move to Renault was on the cards. This started the best spell of Alonso's career as he improved to sixth, then fourth in the Championship before his back-to-back title wins.

Alonso has had somewhat of a nomadic F1 career since then, moving form Renault to McLaren back to Renault, into Ferrari and now back to McLaren and, although his best days are behind him, he is still a fan favourite everywhere he goes.

McLaren Team

STOFFEL VANDOORNE

Factfile

Date of Birth: 26th March 1992
Born: Kortrijk, Belgium
Best-Ever Championship Finish: 20th, 2016
Team: McLaren

Racing Career

AT THE COMPLETELY OPPOSITE end of the experience scale is Fernando Alonso's McLaren teammate Stoofel Vandoorne. The young Belgian is in his first full season in F1 in 2017, with his only previous experience being the 2016 Bahrain Grand Prix where he impressed as an injury stand-in for Alonso; finishing tenth and becoming one of the view drivers to score points in their first-ever Grand Prix.

Vandoorne, like many other F1 drivers, now resides in Monaco and uses this as his base as he jets around the world competing. Vandoorne's rise to F1 has followed the tried and tested footsteps of so many prior, with his career starting in the karting ranks before a move to Formula Renault and then the GP2 series, before his jump to F1. However, it all could have been so different as he only started racing by accident when, whilst accompanying his father on a business trip, he visited a karting track and the owner of the track allowed him to borrow one of the karts.

It was during his Formula Renault days that Vandoorne was first noticed by McLaren, who added them to their young drivers development programme that has also brought through the likes of Lewis Hamilton. This gave Vandoorne the platform to go and build himself an F1 career and it will be interesting to see if the young Belgian can go on from here.

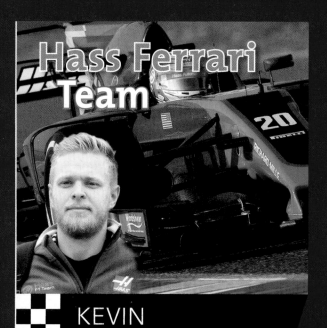

Hass Ferrari Team

MAGNUSSEN

Hass Ferrari Team

🏁 ROMAIN

GROSJEAN

Factfile

Date of Birth: 5th October 1992
Born: Roskilde, Denmark
Best-Ever Championship Finish: 11th, 2014
Team: Haas Ferrari

Factfile

Date of Birth: 26th April 1994
Born: Ufa, Russia
Best-Ever Championship Finish: 7th, 2015
Team: Haas Ferrari

Racing Career

ANOTHER OF THE LONG and illustrious list of Scandinavian drivers in the history of F1 is Danish star Kevin Magnussen. Son of former F1 driver Jens Magnussen, racing was always in Kevin's blood and he started karting at a young age before following the usual routes to F1.

Magnussen has had a stop-start F1 career though after a promising debut year in 2014 which included a second place finish in the Australian Grand Prix, which was his first-ever Grand Prix. This meant that Magnussen became only the second Danish driver to ever score points on his F1 debut; remarkably the other is his father who did it in 1998.The rookie would build on that promising start with 11 further points finishes which earned him 11th place overall in the Championship.

Any hopes he had of building on this the following season were quickly dashed when McLaren announced that former World Champion Fernando Alonso would be rejoining the team and after a year of testing for McLaren (a team he had been with since he was signed up as part of their driver development team as a youngster) he was released from his contract.

The Renault team were quick to snap him up but a frustrating season lay ahead in 2016 with only two points finishes meaning a 16th place finish in the Championship.

It remains to be seen whether Magnussen can recapture the early promise that marked him out as one to watch but at only 25 years old time is still on his side.

Racing Career

ANOTHER OF THE ELDER DRIVERS on the grid comes in the form of French racer Romain Grosjean. Although born in Switzerland Grosjean holds dual French and Swiss nationality and decided to race under the French flag and is currently the only French man in the series. Now a veteran of over 100 Grands Prix, Grosjean is seen as a steady driver who helps his teammates and is a good man to have in the development and practice arenas.

Grosjean is another who went through the usual steps to becoming an F1 star (you will have noticed a trend for most drivers by now so if you want to be an F1 star get yourself to your local karting track as soon as possible!) moving from karting to Formula Renault, then GP2 before the jump to F1 in 2009. This first year in Formula 1 Grosjean was a stand in driver for Renault, where he raced in seven Grands Prix without managing a point. 2010 was to be a year on the sidelines as a test driver before Grosjean was given another chance this time with the Lotus team.

Four years with Lotus was to follow with his best performance being a second place finish in the 2013 USA Grand Prix, this being part of a run of four consecutive podiums in a row that propelled him to his best-ever finish of seventh in the Championship. Grosjean has never managed to reach the heights of the podium again and may be another for whom time is not on their side should he ever wish to be World Champion.

RE
ultimate
27
AULT
Computacenter
GOODWILL
PRIVATE JETS
HECHTER

Facts and Stats

Most World Championships: Michael Schumacher – 7

Youngest World Champion: Sebastian Vettel at 23 years, 134 days old in 2018

Oldest World Champion: Juan Manuel Fangio at 46 years, 41 days old in 1957

Most Race Wins: Michael Schumacher - 91 Wins

Percentage of Races Won: Juan Manuel Fangio - 24 wins in 52 races; 46.15% win rate

Most Wins in a Season: Michael Schumacher - 13 wins

Most Consecutive Wins: Sebastian Vettel - 9 wins

Youngest Winner: Max Verstappen at 18 years, 228 days

Oldest Winner: Luigi Fagioli at 53 years, 22 days

Most Wins in the Same Grand Prix: Michael Schumacher - 8 wins in the French Grand Prix

Most Races Ever: Rubens Barrichello - 322 races

Youngest Driver to Start a Race: Max Verstappen at 17 years, 166 days

Oldest Driver to Start a Race: Louis Chiron at 55 years, 292 days

Most Pole Positions: Michael Schumacher - 68 poles

Most Pole Positions in a Season: Sebastian Vettel - 15 poles

Podium Finishes: Michael Schumacher - 155 podiums

Most Podiums in a Season: Michael Schumacher - 17 podiums

Most Consecutive Podium Finishes: Michael Schumacher - 19 podiums

Most Point Finishes: Michael Schumacher - 221 points finishes

Most Championship Points in a Season: Sebastian Vettel - 397 points in 2013 season

Youngest Drive to Score a Point: Max Verstappen at 17 years, 180 days in the Malaysian Grand Prix, 2015

Oldest Driver to Score Points: Philippe Étancelin at 53 years, 249 days in the Italian Grand Prix, 1950

Most Constructors Championships: Ferrari - 16

Most Constructors Wins: Ferrari - 227

Most Constructors Pole Positions: Ferrari - 210

Most Constructors Podiums: Ferrari - 210

ROLL OF HONOUR
Drivers Championship Winners

YEAR	NATIONALITY	DRIVER	CONSTRUCTOR	YEAR	NATIONALITY	DRIVER	CONSTRUCTOR
1950		Giuseppe Farina [1]	Alfa Romeo	1966		Jack Brabham [5]	Brabham
1951		Juan Manuel Fangio [2]	Alfa Romeo	1967		Denny Hulme [10]	Brabham
1952		Alberto Ascari [3]	Ferrari	1968		Graham Hill [7]	Lotus
1953		Alberto Ascari [3]	Ferrari	1969		Jackie Stewart [11]	Matra
1954		Juan Manuel Fangio [2]	Maserati2	1970		Jochen Rindt [12]	Lotus
1955		Juan Manuel Fangio [2]	Mercedes	1971		Jackie Stewart [11]	Tyrrell
1956		Juan Manuel Fangio [2]	Ferrari	1972		Emerson Fittipaldi [13]	Lotus
1957		Juan Manuel Fangio [2]	Maserati	1973		Jackie Stewart [11]	Tyrrell
1958		Mike Hawthorn [4]	Ferrari	1974		Emerson Fittipaldi [13]	McLaren
1959		Jack Brabham [5]	Cooper	1975		Niki Lauda [14]	Ferrari
1960		Jack Brabham [5]	Cooper	1976		James Hunt [15]	McLaren
1961		Phil Hill [6]	Ferrari	1977		Niki Lauda [14]	Ferrari
1962		Graham Hill [7]	BRM	1978		Mario Andretti [16]	Lotus
1963		Jim Clark [8]	Lotus	1979		Jody Scheckter [17]	Ferrari
1964		John Surtees [9]	Ferrari	1980		Alan Jones [18]	Williams
1965		Jim Clark [8]	Lotus	1981		Nelson Piquet [19]	Brabham

YEAR	NATIONALITY	DRIVER	CONSTRUCTOR	YEAR	NATIONALITY	DRIVER	CONSTRUCTOR
1982		Keke Rosberg[20]	Williams	2000		Michael Schumacher [24]	Ferrari
1983		Nelson Piquet [19]	Brabham	2001		Michael Schumacher [24]	Ferrari
1984		Niki Lauda [14]	McLaren	2002		Michael Schumacher [24]	Ferrari
1985		Alain Prost [21]	McLaren	2003		Michael Schumacher [24]	Ferrari
1986		Alain Prost [21]	McLaren	2004		Michael Schumacher [24]	Ferrari
1987		Nelson Piquet [19]	Williams	2005		Fernando Alonso [28]	Renault
1988		Ayrton Senna [22]	McLaren	2006		Fernando Alonso [28]	Renault
1989		Alain Prost [21]	McLaren	2007		Kimi Räikkönen [29]	Ferrari
1990		Ayrton Senna [22]	McLaren	2008		Lewis Hamilton [30]	McLaren
1991		Ayrton Senna [22]	McLaren	2009		Jenson Button [31]	Brawn
1992		Nigel Mansell [23]	Williams	2010		Sebastian Vettel [32]	Red Bull
1993		Alain Prost [21]	Williams	2011		Sebastian Vettel [32]	Red Bull
1994		Michael Schumacher [24]	Benetton	2012		Sebastian Vettel [32]	Red Bull
1995		Michael Schumacher [24]	Benetton	2013		Sebastian Vettel [32]	Red Bull
1996		Damon Hill [25]	Williams	2014		Lewis Hamilton [30]	Mercedes
1997		Jacques Villeneuve [26]	Williams	2015		Lewis Hamilton [30]	Mercedes
1998		Mika Häkkinen [27]	McLaren	2016		Nico Rosberg [33]	Mercedes
1999		Mika Häkkinen[27]	McLaren				

Quiz Answers

Crossword

(from page 35)

```
                              F I N N I S H  H
          C O U L T H A R D      V E T T E L  U
          L     A                            L
          A     L      S I L V E R S T O N E  K
          R     O              R              E
          K   H U   S H A N G H A I   M   G    N
              U N          I       C   G    B
              N O       M      B    S   I    E
              G F    F   O    U    S   O    R
          G R O S J E A N   T   L   V    G
              A O   R   A Y R T O N S E N N A
              R R   R   C       O   A
              I     A   O   I N D I A   Z
              N     R      B A B   Z
              G     I      A B U D H A B I
```

Wordsearch

(from page 33)

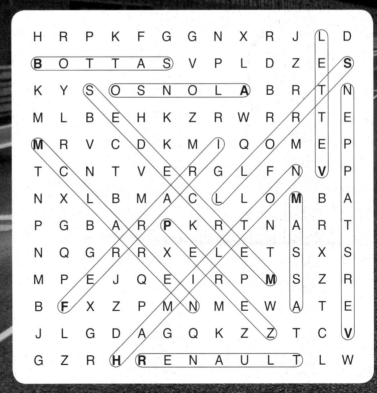

```
H R P K F G G N X R J L D
B O T T A S V P L D Z E S
K Y S O S N O L A B R T N
M L B E H K Z R W R R T E
M R V C D K M I Q O M E P
T C N T V E R G L F N V P
N X L B M A C L L O M B A
P G B A R P K R T N A R T
N Q G R R X E L E T S X S
M P E J Q E I R P M S Z R
B F X Z P M N M E W A T E
J L G D A G Q K Z Z T C V
G Z R H R E N A U L T L W
```

The Big Formula One Quiz

(from page 28)

1. Michael Schumacher
2. Kimi Räikkönen
3. Sebastian Vettel
4. Ten
5. McLaren and Mercedes
6. Max Verstappen and Daniel Ricciardo
7. Monza
8. Nico Rosberg
9. Ferrari
10. 16
11. Australian Grand Prix
12. Lewis Hamilton, Sebastian Vettel,
    Fernando Alonso and Kimi Räikkönen
13. Canadian
14. Ten
15. Four
16. Four
17. Melbourne, Baku, Monaco and Montreal
18. Three
19. Guiseppe Farina
20. 13
21. 2005 and 2006
22. Circuit of the Americas, Texas
23. Belgian
24. Suzuka
25. Max Verstappen
26. Louis Chiron
27. Rubens Barrichello
28. Six
29. Lewis Hamilton and Jacques Villenueve
30. Valtteri Bottas; 231.48 miles per hour

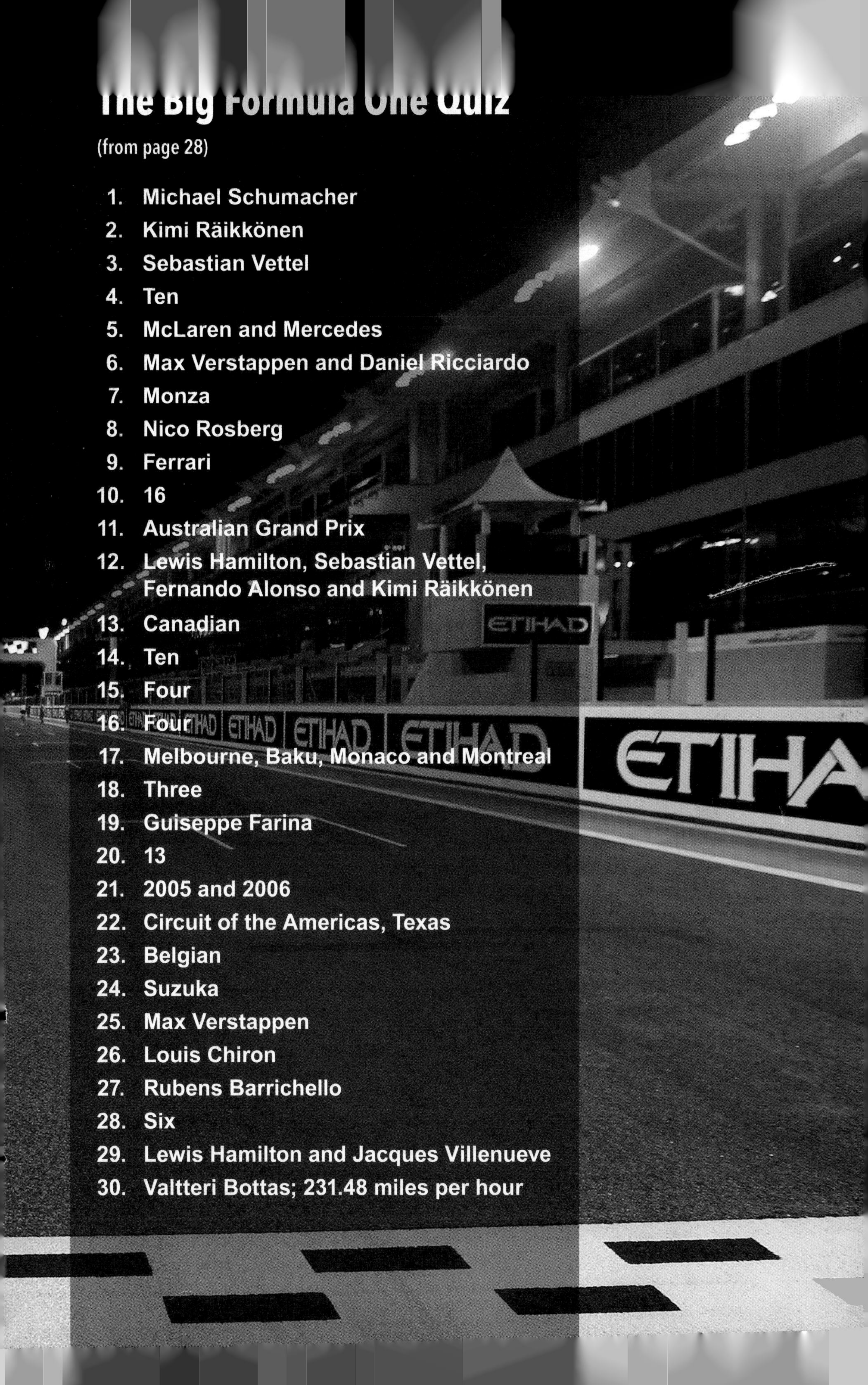

Where's the Driver?